THE FINANCIAL ACTIVIST'S BLUEPRINT

OLOJO CHRISTIANA

Copyright © 2024 Olojo Christiana

All rights reserved.

ISBN: 9798300967727

INTRODUCTION

Welcome to "The Financial Activist's Blueprint: Buy, Build, and Think Your Way to Destiny." In a world where often too little emphasis is being placed on financial literacy and economic disparities are still growing wider, the need for financial activism has never been more crucial. The book is meant to inspire and challenge you to take ownership of your financial future and question the status quo-to become an activist for yourself and your community.

Financial activism is more than personal wealth; financial activism is about an upheaval-a movement that tears down barriers to financial stability and success. It's about understanding how the systems work in our economies and using those understandings to create positive change. Whether one is an aspiring entrepreneur, a seasoned investor, or trying to improve one's financial literacy, this blueprint arms one with the tools and strategies needed for dealing with such a complex financial landscape.

In the pages that follow, you will learn how holistic financial empowerment through three key pillars-Buy, Build, and Think-can be achieved. Each pillar will define the next crucial step on your path to financial independence and activism.

Invest: Learn how to buy with informed decisions that align with your value system and financial goals, educating on the importance of investing into assets that not only grow your wealth but contribute to community health.

Building: Learn how to construct ongoing streams of income and business entities reflective of your passion and mission. This area will walk you through your entrepreneurial journey from ideation to execution, putting much emphasis on the need for resilience and innovation.

Mindset: Think abundance, think empowerment. This would have to do with the psychological aspects of financial success, like challenging your limiting beliefs and being proactive in creating your financial journey.

Throughout this book, you will take away practical advice, real-world examples, and actionable steps to inspire you in taking charge of your financial destiny. You will also find stories of people who have become financial activists-proving that change can indeed happen when we commit to our financial education and advocate for ourselves and others.

As you get started, remember that financial activism is not about the personal bottom line; it is about moving a ripple that can change not only lives but also communities. Embrace your inner financial activist and take a critical role in creating a financial system that is fair and just-one that works for and with all people.

Now, are you ready to take that first concrete step toward financial empowerment? Let's dive into "The Financial Activist's Blueprint" and unlock the potential lying inside. Your destiny awaits!.

CONTENTS

INTRODUCTION

ACKNOWLEDGMENTS

CHAPTER 1: INTRODUCTION TO FINANCIAL ACTIVISM

CHAPTER 2: THE INTELLIGENT INVESTOR MINDSET

CHAPTER 3: UNDERSTANDING THE LANDSCAPE OF FINANCIAL OPPORTUNITIES

CHAPTER 4: BUY THEN BUILD: THE ACQUISITION STRATEGY

CHAPTER 5: THE LEAN START-UP APPROACH

CHAPTER 6: THINK AND GROW: THE POWER OF MINDSET

CHAPTER 7: NAVIGATING VENTURE DEALS

CHAPTER 8: PRIVATE EQUITY DEALS: A DEEPER DIVE

CHAPTER 9: THE MONEY TRAP: RECOGNIZING AND AVOIDING PITFALLS

CHAPTER 10: THE ROLE OF CREDIT INVESTORS

CHAPTER 11: BUILDING A FINANCIAL ACTIVIST NETWORK

CHAPTER 12: WALKING TO DESTINY: CREATING YOUR FINANCIAL LEGACY

CHAPTER 13: TAKING ACTION: YOUR BLUEPRINT FOR SUCCESS

CONCLUSION

ABOUT THE AUTHOR

ACKNOWLEDGMENTS

Insert Today, while reflecting on this journey culminating into the writing of **The Financial Activist's Blueprint: Buy, Build, and Think Your Way to Destiny**, my heart is filled with thankfulness for all those who have stood by me through thick and thin. This will be a testament to collaboration, encouragement, and vision shared between people.

Most importantly, I would like to thank my family. Your continued support and belief in my mission have been my greatest source of strength. Thank you for having patience with the long hours that I put in working on this project, and for always reminding me that at least I needed to chase my passion.

This goes to all those in finance and activism, some of whom have been my mentors and colleagues; to them, I am deeply grateful for their mentorship and wise counsel. Through these people, my perception of how financial systems work and how advocacy plays a much-needed role to bring forth real change were formed. I am grateful to those who have gone out of their way to read my work and provided constructive criticism to streamline my thoughts and helped me strengthen my message.

I also want to acknowledge all of the many, many people and communities I have met along my journey. It was your stories of struggle and perseverance that urged me to write this book. I hope the insights here will help you take your own economic life into your hands and fight for a change in your own life and that of your communities.

To my readers, I would say: thank you for getting this far, and thank you for your interest in financial empowerment. Your interest alone in these ideas moves the concept of economic justice forward. I hope this work will be a great help to you on the road to financial independence and activism.

We can, together, build a future where financial literacy and the power that comes with it truly belongs to all. It has been the highest honor being part of this journey; and I hope that would continue as we buy, build and think our way into a better destiny..

CHAPTER 1
DIVING INTO FINANCIAL ACTIVISM

We all live amidst rapid economic change, social unrest, and environmental hardship. Financial activism is a dynamic expression of positive innovation today, enabling people to take ownership of their financial destinies in support of an equitable and sustainable culture. I will introduce you to financial activism, its underlying philosophy, and give you an overview of what can be expected from this book "The Financial Activist's Blueprint: Buy, Build, and Think Your Way to Destiny."

Define Financial Activism

Financial activism is the deployment of one's financial capability and awareness to become openly active in the pursuit of social, economic, and environmental change. It differs from the traditional notion of investing primarily because it takes into consideration the real impact of financial decisions on communities and the environment. A financial activists realize that actions such as investing, spending, or donating to companies can be a way of promoting justice and sustainability.

It is particularly important in today's world, as wealth disparity and systemic issues plague communities with unrelenting regularity. Financial activism empowers them to make active decisions about their finances-investing in socially responsible businesses, supporting local ventures, or even advocating for legislation promoting equitable economic growth. Financial activism uses money to create a better world, one investment at a time.

That is where the value of financial activism lies when systemic changes can come into place. Financial activists can go a long way in ensuring that corporate behavior changes and the ways of conducting responsible business come forward by investing in companies that observe sustainability, diversity, and ethical business operations. They support the development of resilient communities through the development of local businesses and the fostering of equitable financial policy.

Financial Activist Mindset

To be one, you will need to foster a particular kind of attitude: an activist mindset that is active, educated, and relentless. A certain mindset is distinguished by a set of characteristics including the following:

1. Curiosity and Lifetime Learning

To be one, you will have to commit yourself to lifelong learning. They thoroughly understand that the landscape is complicated and constantly changing; thus, continuous learning about market trends, investment techniques, and economic policy is called for. Their curiosity allows them to make informed decisions.

2. Knowledge is Power

Financial activism is pegged on the understanding that education can change things. They know that personal finance education is the foundation upon which informed choices to realize results are hinged. Empowerment goes past personal finance into teaching others and sharing information within communities.

3. Ideals-Based Decision Making

They invest money based on their ideals; that is, the investment decisions reflect impacts on society and the environment. In respect to this, their actions create constructive corporate and programmatic contributions. Value-based decision-making lets them live their values through their financial activities.

4. Resilience and Adaptability

On days when the market volatility or personal catastrophes that test resolution grind the economy to a crawl, the real financial activist would rise to the occasion by accepting challenges to learn and grow, adjusting course where appropriate, and maneuvering through the often labyrinthine world of high finance.

5. Community Orientation

A financial revolution does not take place in a vacuum. Too often, one's financial situation is closely correlated with the neighborhood they happen to reside in. By pooling resources to fund initiatives, organize local campaigns, or even unite in an attempt to hasten legislative reforms that will benefit society as a whole, perhaps financial activists may be able to achieve even more.

Overview of the Book's Structure and Objectives

This book will be a complete guide for the budding financial activist. Every chapter from now on will take you another step ahead in giving you tools, techniques, and knowledge that will help you go through the financial maze without losing your soul.

All the chapters will review the principles of smart investing, laying the foundation for an informed choice, show you the big picture of financial opportunities and how to be prepared to identify and seize them. The buy-then-build strategy will be explored in detail on how to acquire and improve assets to achieve long-term growth. I will also delve into the lean start up model which will be discussed in detail on how to become agile and creative with financial undertakings.

More chapter will explain in detail the key themes of the book: the development of mindset; how to handle venture and private equity deals; how to avoid financial pitfalls; and how to build your network and finally, the last chapter will give you a step-by-step action plan to help you implement the methods outlined in this book.

The intent of this book is to inform and inspire your action. By the end of this journey, you'll know exactly how to take concrete action to become a financial activist-one who buys, builds, and thinks strategically to create a future that reflects your values and goals.

We begin this journey together, and remember financial activism is more about the means to a wealth accumulation end; it's a means to using your wealth in constructive change. It's making the journey down the path to financial empowerment with purpose and intention. Let's take the first step toward your goals..

CHAPTER 2
MIND OF AN INVESTOR

To lead in long-term success in financial activism, You will have to educate your mindset as an investor. When discussing intelligent investing concepts, the role and process of research and due diligence in fundamental investment philosophies, the tactics to make appropriate financial decisions. You will, therefore, be ready to allow complexity into the world of finance and align your assets with values by adopting the intelligent investor attitude.

Understand The Concept of Intelligent Investing.

Intelligent investing involves more than the pursuit of profit alone, it is a responsible means toward growth over the long term, assuming calculated risks, and accountability. Following are some basic principles which define the intelligent investor's mindset:

1. Value Investing
Legendary investors like Benjamin Graham and Warren Buffett have talked lengthily on this subject. Essentially, this is when one identifies undervalued assets that may appreciate considerably over time which may come in stocks, bonds, or even real estate. Value investors do not look at the market price an asset has but look at its intrinsic value and look at opportunities whereby the market has mispriced the investment.

2. Margin of Safety

The first and foremost investment lesson is the "margin of safety." It is basically a difference between what an asset intrinsically is worth and the price at which actually the asset trades in the market. If a person has invested with a margin of safety, he will be safeguarded from the uncertainty of the market and/or possible losses. That means estimates should be conservative, and one must look for investments that could give some cushion to the risk.

3. Long-Term Orientation

They discipline themselves to think long and avoid the somewhat wild fluctuations that the markets have in the short run. He is always resisting the frequent feeling to immediately act upon changes in market conditions, his eyes are always on the core value of his investments. It is this patience that allows him to bear the decline in the market and grab an opportunity to buy at a value when everybody else is panicking.

4. Diversification

Risk handling can be done by diversification. They diversify their investments across classes of assets, sectors, and geographic regions for lessened consequences of poor performance in any single investment in the overall portfolio. You thereby form a view that you should not put all your eggs into one basket for security in your financial future.

5. Emotional Discipline

They also call for emotional discipline. Though processes can be adversely affected by fear and greed, which climax into poor investment decisions. He will nurture emotional resilience and stick to a clearly defined investment strategy whereby he avoids speculation in the market and makes rational choices based on sound and quality research and analysis.

The Importance of Research and Due Diligence

Research and due diligence are absolutely indispensable in intelligent investing. The better informed you are with regards to your investments, the more capable you'll be at making correct decisions. Here is why these practices are important:

1. Grasping the Investment Landscape

An extensive research gives you insight into the markets, something very important as it gave a view on market trends, economic indicators, and the dynamics of industries. Such knowledge will enable you to identify possible opportunities and further assess their viability. Be it in stocks, bonds, real estate, or alternative investments, understanding the landscape is salient to making informed choices.

2. Financial Health

This also concerns the financial health of prospective investments. For stocks, that includes examining financial statements, earnings reports, and key performance indicators. Real estate involves assessing property values, rental income potential, and market conditions. The financial health of any investment stands to better help you place its growth potential and risk.

3. Identifying Risks

Every investment has some inherent risks. Research will help you identify the present risk and understand the same so that a decision to invest or not in that instrument can be taken with due consideration. In addition, it involves the study of market volatility, regulatory changes, and economic factors that may affect the performance of your investment.

4. Being Informed

Everything changes and being informed is actually the intelligent thing to do while investing. News, market reports, and economic indicators should be regularly considered to adjust your strategy to meet the changing circumstances. Only this proactive approach will make you privy to opportunities and threats that may arise.

Key Investment Philosophies and Strategies

Learning some of the principal investment ideas and techniques will help you make better judgments as you start to develop your intelligent investor mentality. The following summary mentioned below are some of the keys and ideas.

1. Growth Investing

Investment in businesses that are growing-as often reflected by rising profits and revenues. The price of stocks that growth investors feel will outperform the market in the long run always remains high. This kind of investment often entails much higher levels of risk and volatility, although the returns can be very impressive.

2. Income Investing

This is a strategy underlining the need for regular income through investments in the form of dividends or interest payments. To such investors who look ahead to creating wealth and achieving financial freedom, this will be pretty appealing. A usual favorite of income investors are bonds, REITs with assured returns, and equities that pay dividends.

3. Socially Responsible Investment

Here, the financial activist reaches complete or fuller alignment of values. SRI would be the exemplary case of how to integrate social, ethical, and ecological criteria into the investment decision-making process. Support companies that lead in sustainability, diversity, and corporate social responsibility, and one will concurrently profit and be provided for.

4. Impact Investing

In this, like SRI, the stakes go a notch higher to create financial returns with a positive social and environmental impact. Impact investors look to conduct business and invest in ventures that tend to solve pressing human needs like housing, healthcare access, and renewable energy.

5. Quantitative Investing

Using this investment method, the investor depends on an algorithm and a mathematical model to decide where he or she should invest. To detect patterns and trends that could help make investment decisions, quantitative investors need to consider huge amounts of data. Although this might be quite a successful technique, it also requires proficiency in two main areas(Technology and Data Analysis).

6. Value Averaging

This is when the total amount of money invested at any given moment depends on the performance of that particular asset. Instead, in value averaging, investing when prices are low and less when they are high, as opposed to setting aside a certain sum of money at fixed periods, is suggested. This investment strategy may be regarded as one of the ways of reducing risk and getting greater profits in the end.

Remember, informed choices and the resolution to bring investments in line with principles form the foundation of financial activism.

CHAPTER 3
UNDERSTANDING THE DIFFERENT FINANCIAL LANDSCAPE

In general, knowledgeable investment decisions, in confluence with values and goals, call for deep knowledge of the diverse landscape that exists regarding financial opportunities. The chapter shall review several investment types such as stock, real estate, private equity, and venture capital, further discussing current trends in markets and how to identify opportunities. The concept of risk management will also be discussed. By the end of this chapter, you will be better placed to understand what the investment landscape really looks like and what is required in terms of tools to navigate through it effectively.

An Introduction to Investment Types: Analyzing Stocks, Bonds, ETFs, Mutual Funds, and Real Estate

Stocks

Stocks are ownership in firms and happen to be one of the most common types of investment. Ownership in a firm comes right from buying its shares, which entitle the investor to a share of the profit or loss the company generates. Basically, there are two types of stocks: common and preferred. Common stocks come with voting rights and capital appreciation; holders of preferred stocks enjoy fixed dividends, though, and a higher claim on assets in the case of liquidation.

- *Advantages*: The return on equity can be very high, particularly for the long-term investor. They are relatively liquid securities since investors can readily buy and sell the ownership in stock exchanges.

- *Disadvantages:* Stock prices may fluctuate immensely depending on market sentiment, economic conditions, and results posted by the company. This may very well translate into huge short-term losses.

2. Real Estate

Real estate investment involves the buying of property with an eye toward earning rental income or capital appreciation. Within this broad class of assets come residential, commercial, and industrial properties. Real estate is a tangible investment, offering a sense of security and stability.

- *Positives:* Real estate is a source of passive income through rents and probably appreciation over the long term. Real estates provide tax benefits like depreciation deductions and mortgage interest.

- *Negatives:* Real estate investment requires substantial capital. Involves in some occasions ongoing expenses related to maintenance and property administration. Sometimes, the market is in liquid. Selling real estate properties is very difficult.

3. Private Equity

Private equity investment involves investing in privately held companies or the buying out of public companies to delist them from stock exchanges. Private equity firms generally raise funds from accredited investors and institutional investors for the acquisition and management of such companies.

- *Advantages:* private equity investments may return profits brought in since firms usually realize operational improvements and strategic changes which, taken together, will result in enhanced firm value. The investors also acquire the unique opportunities to invest in companies that are not available publicly.

- **_Disadvantages:_** private equity investments are normally illiquid, with your capital locked up for some years. Risks involved are also higher since the success of the investment is under the talent of the management team to execute their strategy.

4. Venture Capital

Venture capital is a subgroup of private equity investment directed at early-stage companies with high growth prospects. In venture capital, money is given for equity, and the venture capitalist often assumes an active role in the development of the company.

- **_Advantages:_** Venture capital may yield high returns once a firm enjoys success, since early investors in the company can earn great equity appreciation. Secondly, venture capitalists usually gain a position through which they can influence the direction of the firm.

- **_Disadvantages:_** Investments in venture capital are by nature risky due to the fact that most startups fail. Investors might suffer from long holding periods before realizing returns, since most startups take years to mature.

Discussion on Market Trends: How to Find Opportunities

Market trends can quite helpfully lead one to spot the exact investment opportunities. Some of the following are important to monitor along with observing the potential investments:

1. Economic Leading Indicators

GDP growth, rate of unemployment, rate of inflation, and consumer confidence are good economic indicators. These leading indicators give insight into the health of an economy and also give warning of impending investment opportunities. For example, a growing economy is reflected by increased consumer spending in retail and services.

2. Technological Changes

The rapid development of technologies at a fast pace opens new vistas in different industries. Fintech, health tech, and renewable energy-related businesses are in the fast growth path owing to unexpected growth in technologies. Awareness about upcoming technologies will help in learning about the companies that have bright future prospects.

3. Demographic Shifts

Changes in demographics could include aging of the population or urbanization trends, either of which might provide investment opportunities. Indeed, the growing demand for health services and senior living facilities not only creates opportunities in healthcare but also crosses over into the real estate sector.

4. Sustainability and ESG Investing

Forces of nature such as environmental and social concerns, and aspects of governance, are increasingly material to investors. More often than not, such companies committed to sustainability and social responsibility emerge as the most successful even well into the future. Value alignment with your portfolio, capitalize on market trends, and ESG-compliant investments are some of the reasons why.

5. Market Sentiment

Knowing the market sentiment means basically knowing the attitude and feelings of investors. It sometimes creates an opportunity for you. Sometimes, market sentiments force the market to undervalue or overvalue an asset. By interpreting various sentiment indicators like consumer surveys and market volatility, you may make informed investment decisions.

Introduce the Concept of Risk Management

The key to successful investing is risk management. It is a process whereby you first identify risks that could affect your investments; second, you assess such risks; and third, you take mitigating measures against those risks. Following are some principles of risk management.

1. Diversification

The ideal way to manage risk is through diversification. In that, the investment can be held in a variety of asset classes, sectors, and geographic regions. By doing so, no single factor of poor performance would substantially affect the overall portfolio. Diversity helps in stabilizing return with minimum loss.

2. Asset Allocation

It is an intentional spreading of your investments across asset classes, which include equities, fixed income securities, real estate, and cash. Your asset allocation should be consistent with your risk tolerance, investment objectives, and time horizon. Balanced asset allocation aids one in attaining financial goals with controlled risk.

3. Monitor and Rebalance

The world of investments moves very fluidly, and regular monitoring of one's portfolio is a matter of ultimate importance. Every now and then go through your investments with the view of ensuring that they are in concert with your goals and risk tolerance. This would involve adjustment in the allocation of the assets with a view to getting you back to the desired risk profile.

4. Stop-Loss Orders

Such a type of order would automatically trigger a sell when an asset has reached a certain, predetermined price. At its very core, as the risk management strategy, it is used to limit losses and protect your capital in conditions of very high volatility. While this cannot avoid the risk totally, it will be some kind of cushion during market reversals.

5. Know your Risk Appetite

The greater the amount of risk an investor can tolerate, the higher the return that one may get. Age, financial position, and investment goals-all combine to tell what your risk tolerance is. Knowing your risk tolerance may make a big difference in the way you go about taking investment decisions. Know how you are 'comfortable' with the market fluctuations and shape your investment accordingly.

The financial activist knows the financial opportunity landscape. By knowing the various types of investments, such as stocks, real estate, private equity, and venture capital, one will identify ideal opportunities that correspond with one's values and goals. This will enable one to deal with risk in an appropriate manner since the trends of the market will be well in step to go through the various complexities with confidence.

CHAPTER 4
BUY THEN BUILD: THE ACQUISITION STRATEGY

The buy then build approach is a very powerful vehicle for financial activism that creates value and provokes change. This chapter is intended to present case studies of successful buy-then-build strategies, and discuss how to spot undervalued assets and businesses. By your understanding of this acquisition strategy, you will be able to foster personal success through financial resources while making communities and industries better in the process.

Explaining the Buy-Then-Build Approach to Investing

The buy-then-build strategy of investment means a process whereby an investor buys already existing businesses or assets and then adds value to them through initiatives touching on operational improvements, strategic initiatives, and innovation. This approach is contrasted with startup investing, whereby entrepreneurs initiate business from scratch. Rather, buy-then-build focuses on leveraging existing resources and infrastructure to drive growth in profitability.

Key aspects of the buy-then-build approach include:

1. Established Assets Acquisition
This strategy involves the identification and acquisition of

established businesses or assets that need improvement. The undervaluation in their price might be a result of mismanagement, market conditions, or lack of innovation.

2. Operational Improvement

The second stage is operational value increment after takeover. The much-vaunted process reengineering, product or product mix enhancement, supply chain rationalization, or customer service improvements are some ways of improving operations to achieve better efficiency and profitability.

3. Strategic Growth Initiatives

This involves those where the company will expand into new areas, diversification of product lines, or deploy technology for competitive advantage. This readies the asset to realize full value through growth.

4. Value Creation

In the long run or at least focuses less on the short-term benefits that can be derived. Thus, investors may, through a focus on growth over the long term and quality in operations, be able to build firms that benefit themselves and serve the community.

Discussing How to Identify Undervalued Assets and Businesses

The number one profound skill of any successful buy-then-build investor is the ability to find undervalued assets and businesses. The following strategies may help you find such an opportunity:

1. Financial Analysis

Deep financial analysis is, in fact, the very heart of finding undervalued assets. Look for firms with solid underpinnings-low debt, good cash flow, and decent profit margins-that are not reflected correctly in their share prices owing to some temporal or market sentiment-induced problems. Key financial indicators to consider include P/E ratios, price-to-book, and return on equity.

2. Market Research

Understand the market trends and industrial dynamics that would help in uncovering businesses undervalued rather than their peers. Research the growth or transformation phases that sectors undergo, as this might highlight an opportunity. Check for businesses that have operational flaws but are well-recognized brands.

3. Networking and Relationships

A relationship with industry insiders, business brokers, and financial advisors will most definitely yield acquisition prospects. Networking can help you uncover opportunities that may well not be publicly listed or widely known.

4. Distressed Assets

It could be a business or other assets that run into financial distress, operational challenges, or a market decline. Higher-risk investments, these carry with them serious upside potential, should you be able to implement successful turnaround strategies.

5. Leverage Technology

Employ technology and data analytics to find trends and opportunities. Use financial modeling software, market analysis platforms, and business intelligence to uncover undervalued assets that may possess hidden value in waiting to be improved.

Case Studies of Successful Buy-Then-Build Strategies

It would be instructive to first consider a few case studies of successful investors and companies that applied the buy-then-build strategy:

1. Berkshire Hathaway and Geico

Probably the most famous buy-then-build example involves Warren Buffett's Berkshire Hathaway. In 1996, Berkshire took control of an auto insurance company called Geico that, at the time of purchase, was reporting weak earnings. Buffett saw value in the good growth prospects and Geico's brand. After the acquisition, Berkshire implemented several cost improvements, process simplifications, and advertising efforts. For this reason, Geico became one of the United States' largest auto insurers and became a meaningful contributor to Berkshire's overall performance.

2. The Home Depot and HD Supply

As the largest home improvement retailer, The Home Depot

chased the buy-the-build strategy when it acquired HD Supply back in 2007. HD Supply previously was a distributor of construction and maintenance products but also underperformed for quite some time. After acquisition, The Home Depot pursued improvements in operation, alignment of supply chains, and customer service. HD Supply would enable The Home Depot to further expand its product suite and entrench a leading market position, which would have obvious implications for growing revenues and profitability for the business.

3. Thryfty and the Thrift Store Model

Thryfty, a social enterprise focused on sustainability and community support, adopted a buy-then-build approach through the acquisition of sick thrift stores across regions. Operational efficiencies such as improved inventory management and more effective marketing have allowed Thryfty to renew these stores to profitability. The organization also engaged in community outreach by giving a share of profits to local charities. In this business model, it doesn't just add value to the financial performance of the shops but also to society.

4. Kraft Heinz

Acquisition of Kraft Foods Perhaps the most recent possible example of a buy-then-build strategy is that between Kraft Foods and Heinz in 2015. After the merger, the combined company looked at operational efficiencies, cost-cutting measures, and product innovation. Kraft Heinz could achieve streamlined operations with the strengths of both brands at its helm-positive for growth and profitability in a very competitive marketplace.

Perhaps the most powerful strategy available in creating value and effecting positive change for the financial activist investor is the buy-and-build method. It is here that the full investment potential can be unlocked through the acquisition of undervalued assets and businesses, effecting operational improvements, and then pursuing strategic growth initiatives.

Also, as you go through this financial activism, the buy-then-build strategy allows you not only to be personally financially successful but also to have a real say in the businesses and communities you invest in.

CHAPTER 5
LEAN START-UP APPROACH

The world of finance and entrepreneurship is such that at all costs, one should be able to innovate and adapt with quick changes. The lean start-up approach involves a formidable methodology that focuses acutely on efficiency, customer feedback, and iterative development. It was this chapter that would introduce the lean start-up methodology, discuss the application of lean principles to financial activism, and explore how agility and adaptability are two imperatives within investment. Embracing such concepts will help one improve on investment strategies and create some real impact on their financial ventures.

An Introduction to Lean Start-Up Methodology

The lean start-up methodology is a systematic approach to building and running a startup by applying the core principles of waste reduction to achieve maximum learning. Key lean start-up methodology principles include

1. Build-Measure-Learn Feedback Loop

The heart of the lean start-up methodology is an effective build-measure-learn feedback loop. This iterative process invites the entrepreneur to swiftly create a minimum viable product, launch it into the market for testing, gather feedback, and make informed adjustments. It thereby aims at learning from real customers and refining one's product or service based on that feedback.

2. Validated Learning

The Lean startup takes validated learning as a principle because it tests either the business model or the product hypotheses through experiments. In collecting data by analyzing customers' responses, the entrepreneurs will see what works or doesn't to make a pivot or persevere based on evidence rather than assumptions.

3. Minimum Viable Product

The minimum viable product represents a version from which a product has just the necessary features to satisfy early adopters. Employing an MVP means an entrepreneur enters the market as quickly as possible, is able to get feedback right away, and also works out a better offering without investing too much at the beginning.

4. Pivot or Pervere

Based on the insights related to the build-measure-learn loop, the entrepreneur decides whether to make a fundamental change in the product or business model or continue on the present path. This is very crucial for decision-making and trying to adapt to the demand of the market for long-term success.

Panel Discussion: Implementing Lean Principles into Financial Activism

The lean start-up methodology can be used very effectively in financial activism to help an investor make informed decisions with a minimum of risk while maximizing impact. Following are some ways you can apply lean principles to your financial activism:

1. Make MVP Investments

Just like the lean start-up that starts with an MVP, a financial activist too can start by investing money-but only a small amount-into either projects or companies reflecting values in congruence with his. This way, you invest less money and test the waters concerning the viability of your investment before you decide on bigger sums of money. You get insight into what works and what does not without putting yourself at great risk.

Market Research and Idea Validation

Do thorough market research before investing your money. The investor needs to make sure that the ideas are assessed and assumptions are validated in depth through potential customers, stakeholders, and other industry experts. Thereby, he could get better insights into the landscapes and choose opportunities that would best fit his goals of financial activism, hence reducing the tendency to invest in failing ventures.

3. Iterate Based on Feedback

After you have invested, proactively seek to understand the views of stakeholders, customers, and the community. These should serve to refine investment strategy and underpin informed decisions about future investments. The openness to input and the readiness to adapt will add value to financial activism overall.

4. Measure Impact and Success

Clearly define metrics that shall help to understand how well your money is working for you. It may be financial return, social impact, or environmental sustainability. Monitoring of these metrics will show how well your money serves you and will help in making decisions based on data for future deployment.

5. Foster a culture of experimentation-invest with a mindset of experimentation

Be prepared to try new strategies, unusual opportunities, learn from success and failures. The culture of experimentation will allow you to move along with market changes and grab emerging opportunities.

Exploring the Importance of Agility and Adaptability in Investments

In modern financial times, agility and adaptability are qualities no investor can afford to compromise on. Here is why this quality is so important:

1. Speedy Market Changes

Financial markets are prone to several influences that include economic changes, technological advancement, and consumer preference alteration. In such a scenario, the investor who is capable of adapting fast can make use of the newer opportunities that may come out and reduce the potential risks.

2. Reaction to Feedback

Lean startups take customer feedback for the improvement of their products. Much on similar lines, it is much expected from investors to be responsive to the market signals and inputs by the stakeholders. Active listening to feedback and making changes in strategies can help to augment investment outcome and hence, keep your portfolio aligned with the dynamic demands of the marketplace.

3. Dealing with Uncertainty

The financial world is essentially filled with uncertainty, with events like the collapse of economies, changing regulatory environments, and geopolitical movements occurring unexpectedly. Such agility in strategy allows investors to change course as unexpected challenges arise, thereby making them resilient against reverses.

4. Continuous Learning

Agility stimulates a continuous learning process in which the investor is encouraged to seek knowledge, analyze data, and stay informed of trends in the industry. This commitment to learning will enable you to make informed decisions, modifying investment strategies in time with state-of-the-art insights.

5. Building Resilient Portfolios

You can build a resilient portfolio that holds good under the stress of the market. Diversification of investments and an open mindset to new opportunities create a well-rounded portfolio-a portfolio that minimizes risks and maximizes potential return.

The Lean start-up approach provides a set of insights and methodologies that can add great value to your financial activism. With lean thinking, including the build-measure-learn feedback loop, validated learning, and the MVP, comes a reasoned approach to investment decisions in creating value in your vision and change.

Agility and adaptability are the qualities that can bring about far-reaching changes in the complex maze of the financial world. The three steps toward getting it are: stay receptive to feedback, learn constantly, and be willing to make a shift in the direction taken when the time is right. This again will create better investment strategies and meaningful impact.

CHAPTER 6
THINK AND GROW: THE POWER OF MINDSET

What plays a very significant role in this journey of success financially and as an activist is not just simple knowledge of the markets or strategies of investment, but something more deep-rooted-mindset. The way one thinks about money, success, and his or her potential can act as a serious determinant toward his or her financial outcomes. This chapter reviews the role of mindset in financial success, presents some techniques for developing a growth mindset, and introduces a few visualization and goal-setting methods that may help one move closer to achieving his or her financial goals.

The Role of Mindset in Financial Success

It means a set of beliefs and attitudes that influence the way we look at ourselves and at what happens in life. As far as financial success is concerned, mindset does all it can to determine the way one takes up challenges, opportunities, and setbacks. Herein comes the following:

1. Money Beliefs

Your thinking about money empowers or limits you. A poverty mindset is based upon a belief of not having enough, leading to fear and anxiety and missed opportunities. On the other side, an abundance mindset embraces the belief of ample resources; you would take calculated risks to pursue opportunities.

2. Resilience in the Face of Challenges

A positive mindset is what helps you look at challenges as opportunities to grow, not as something impossible. So when one faces a challenge-in the case of a setback, an individual with a growth mindset is very much capable of learning from their experiences, altering their strategies, and persisting through such sets of circumstances. Financial activism has many ups and downs that require this resilience.

3. Openness to Learning

A disposition characterized by learning and curiosity permits constant learning, knowing, and skill-building. Such openness is particularly important in the unending evolution in the financial world; new trends, technologies, and strategies pop up rather often. In building a disposition which nurtures lifelong learning, you position yourself right at the forefront of grasping those opportunities in the course of development.

4. Confidence and Self-efficacy

Your attitude represents your self-efficacy, that is, those beliefs in your capability to successfully complete a course of action, such as attaining financial goals. A firm sense of self-efficacy builds motivation to take action and make decisions while chasing your financial objectives with certainty. The lack of confidence, on the other hand, occasions various cases of hesitation and missed opportunities.

5. Decision-Making

Your mindset can even affect the way you go about making decisions. With a fixed mindset, you will avoid taking risks because you will not want to fail, while with a growth mindset, experimentation and innovation will be encouraged. Smart, confident decision-making is a big part of successful investing and financial activism.

Growth Mindset Building Techniques

Developing a growth mindset is going to be majorly important for your financial success and learning to actually welcome challenges.

Here are some ways this may be done:

1. Embrace Challenges

Instead of avoiding challenges, seek them out. Opportunities for growth and learning should not be looked upon as roadblocks but rather as chances to learn and grow. If you are in a tough situation, ask immediately, "What am I going to learn from this, and what am I able to improve?".

2. Reframe Failure

Change your mindset about failure. What if, instead of failure being an outcome, it were actually a good learning curve? Analyze what went wrong, identify the lessons learned from this particular project, and use that insight for future endeavors. After all, many successful investors and entrepreneurs have faced failures before their eventual success.

3. Practice self-compassion

Be gentle with yourself if there are setbacks. Everybody makes mistakes, and nothing comes overnight; that is how growth happens. The practice of self-compassion allows an individual to keep their thinking positive and motivates them to go further.

4. Surround yourself with growth-oriented people

The surroundings mean a lot. Find yourself mentors, peers, and communities that instill a growth mindset within you. Engage yourself in discussions that will challenge the way you think and give you more aspirations to expand your thinking.

5. Set Learning Goals

Other than financial goals, set certain learning goals. Pinpoint the areas where you want to improve your knowledge or skillset, then make a plan to get those goals. This focus on learning will reinforce a growth mindset and keep you going.

Introducing Visualization and Goal Setting

Visualization and goal setting are two of the powerful techniques that will help you crystallize your financial aspirations into reality and strengthen your positive mindset. Here's how to effectively apply these strategies:

1. Visualization

This is a process of visualization whereby you visualize your goals and the ways of reaching them. The motivation and focus can be enhanced through this technique. Here's how one can practice visualization.

- *Create a Vision Board:* Gather pictures, quotes, and symbols that speak to your financial goals and wants. Place them on a board or online at a location where you can review them daily. The visual reminds one of what they are working toward.

- *Daily Practice of Visualization:* These include practicing every day and visualizing your goals. Just close your eyes and imagine yourself reaching these financial goals. Visualize the feelings, things you are going to do, and how it will affect you. This practice reinforces commitment and helps one stay focused on their objectives.

2. SMART Goal-Setting

Setting clear, actionable goals is the best way to make your aspirations real. Effective goals can be set using the SMART criteria:

- *Specific:* Specify exactly what you want to achieve. Instead of saying, "I want to invest more," say, "I want to invest $5,000 in socially responsible companies by the end of the year."

- *Measurable:* Set criteria to measure your progress. This would allow you to keep track of achievements that may help one stay motivated.

- *Achievable:* Your goals should be realistic and achievable. Consider what resources, skills, and timescales you have for your goals.

- ***Relevant:*** Your goals should align with your values and long-term vision. Make sure your financial goals help you reach your big mission as a financial activist.

- ***Time-bound:*** The need to achieve the set goals should be bound by a deadline. This instills a sense of urgency and helps you stay focused on your goals.

3. Periodic Review and Re-evaluation

Give special time to the periodic review of your goals and achievements. Recognize each small success and think about what exactly was an obstacle to your reaching your goal. Refine those goals in accordance with life changes and your expanded insight about what works best for you. This way, you are going to further solidify your commitments toward growth and agility.

Mindset is absolutely crucial in financial success and activism. You can overcome obstacles through a growth mindset by embracing challenges and being compassionate to yourself; then, visualize and strategize solutions that will help actualize your wants while you stay connected with your journey. As you continue to create more in your financial activist blueprint, remember one of the key drivers of your success: mindset.

CHAPTER 7
NAVIGATING VENTURE DEALS

Venture deals represent that juncture when innovation meets capital. For the financial activist-that is to say, one who would not only build wealth but also affect meaningful change-knowing how to navigate such deals matters. This chapter will take you through sourcing and evaluating venture deals, negotiation tactics, insight into deal structuring, and some common pitfalls to avoid along the way.

Sourcing and Evaluating Venture Deals

1. Understanding the Landscape

The first thing to do in sourcing venture deals is getting oriented with the ecosystem. This involves an idea of the kind of ventures that attract investment, for example, technology, health, or sustainable ventures. Go to industry conferences, networking events, and pitch competitions to meet entrepreneurs and other investors. Online platforms such as AngelList and Crunchbase will also give a good overview of the emerging companies and trends.

2. Network

Your network is your most powerful resource in finding deals. Build a network of contacts including entrepreneurs, other investors, and business experts in your desired niche. Again, you can do this by joining venture capital investment groups or clubs. Interacting with your diversified network will not only provide access to potential deals but also offer various perspectives in the ways of looking at opportunities.

3. Opportunity Evaluation

After sourcing potential deals, the next step will be evaluation. Key components of this include:

- *Market Analysis:* Market size and growth potential and competitive landscape, if any. A great market usually precedes a great venture.

- *Business Model:* Explain how the company will make money. Can the business model be scaled? Is there a well-defined path to profitability?

- *Team Assessment:* The founding team experience and skills are assessed along with their track record. In most instances, a good, committed team is the backbone of any successful venture.

- *Financial Projections:* Go through the company's financial projections and historical performance. Are these projections realistic? What assumptions are they based on?

- *Due Diligence:* Perform extensive due diligence that could help to unravel many potential red flags. This includes legal, financial, and operational assessments.

Negotiation Tactics and Deal Structuring

1. Preparing for Negotiation

Preparation is the key to successful negotiation. Understand your objectives and value will be brought in by you. Know your limits and be ready to walk away if the terms do not align with your goals. Understand what motivates the other party in order to find common interests.

2. Establishing Terms

In structuring a deal, the following elements may be considered:

- *Valuation:* Agree on the reasonable valuation of the company. This usually tends to be one of the most knotty issues in the whole negotiation. Comparable company analysis and market trends may be used to support your argument.

- *Equity Stake:* The percentage of equity you will have in return for your investment. It should essentially be a reflection of the risk that you are going to take and your possible upside.

- *Control and Governance:* Deciding on the level of control in the company requires your consideration. Will you be given a seat on the board? What are your voting rights?

- *Exit Strategy:* Discuss the potential exit strategy upfront. Having a clear exit plan-through acquisition, IPO, or whatever method-can make decisions at later stages easier to make.

3. Effective Negotiation Tactics

- *Active Listening:* Listening is also important as speaking. Understand the other party's needs and also what the major problems are so that mutually beneficial solutions can be found.

- *Be Transparent:* Honesty helps in building trust. Be clear about intentions and expectations.

- *Use Leverage Wisely:* If you have multiple offers or strong alternatives, use this leverage to negotiate better terms. However, avoid being overly aggressive; this will burn relationships.

- *Be Flexible:* Be open to creative solutions that might not have been considered at the beginning. Flexibility can result in both sides winning.

Common Pitfalls and How to Avoid Them

1. Overvaluing Opportunities

The common mistake made in a venture deal is overvaluation of a company because of hype rather than being fundamental-based. Do not get carried away with excitement. Always depend on data and well-researched information whenever making a decision.

2. Ignoring Due Diligence

Poor due diligence or rushing through it leads to costly mistakes later on. Give yourself time to conduct a proper review of the financials, legal standing, and operational practices of the company. The step is important in discovering potential risks.

3. Poor Definition of Roles and Responsibilities

Ambiguity in roles breeds conflicts down the road. Clearly define the responsibilities of all parties involved in the deal to ensure accountability and alignment.

4. Neglecting Post-Investment Engagement

Investing in a venture doesn't end with a deal. Continue to be part of the company post-investment by providing support, mentorship, and resources to scale the business. This may further enhance the success of your investment and even your friendship with founders.

5. Not Appreciating Cultural Fit

And where there is a culture mismatch, friction can create impediments to progress. Take some time to gauge whether your values mesh with the company and the founders' values. If the cultural fit is strong, collaboration will go much easier and will help assure success.

In-conclusion, Doing venture deals is an art and a science. By understanding the sourcing and evaluation process, negotiating skills, and how to prepare for common pitfalls in this sector, you will be well on your way to becoming a smart investor and financial activist.

CHAPTER 8
PRIVATE EQUITY DEALS: A DEEPER DIVE

Private equity (PE) investing represents a powerful avenue for financial activists seeking to create significant impact while generating substantial returns. Unlike public markets, private equity involves investing directly in private companies or buying out public companies to delist them from stock exchanges. This chapter will explore the world of private equity investing, discuss the lifecycle of a private equity deal, and analyze case studies of successful private equity investments.

Exploring the World of Private Equity Investing

1. What is Private Equity?

Private equity refers to investment funds that acquire equity ownership in private companies or public companies with the intent to take them private. These investments are typically made by institutional investors, high-net-worth individuals, and specialized private equity firms. The goal is to improve the financial performance of the acquired companies and eventually sell them for a profit, often within a timeframe of 4 to 7 years.

2. Types of Private Equity Investments

Private equity encompasses various strategies, including:

- **Buyouts:** Acquiring a controlling interest in a company, often using a combination of debt and equity. This can include leveraged buyouts (LBOs), where significant debt is used to finance the acquisition.

- **Growth Capital:** Investing in mature companies looking for capital to expand or restructure operations without changing control of the business.

- **Venture Capital:** A subset of private equity focused on early-stage companies with high growth potential. While often considered separately, venture capital is a crucial part of the private equity landscape.

- **Distressed Investments:** Acquiring companies that are underperforming or facing financial difficulties, with the aim of turning them around.

3. The Role of Private Equity Firms

Private equity firms play a critical role in the investment process. They typically raise funds from investors, conduct due diligence on potential acquisitions, and actively manage the portfolio companies to enhance their value. These firms often have specialized expertise in various industries, allowing them to implement strategic changes that drive growth.

The Lifecycle of a Private Equity Deal

Understanding the lifecycle of a private equity deal is essential for financial activists looking to navigate this complex landscape. The process can be broken down into several key stages:

1. Fundraising

First step in the lifecycle is raising capital from investors. Private equity firms create funds that pool money from institutional investors, family offices, and high-net-worth individuals. The firm outlines its investment strategy, target returns, and the types of companies it plans to acquire.

2. Sourcing Deals

Once the fund is established, the firm begins sourcing potential investment opportunities. This involves networking, leveraging industry contacts, and conducting market research to identify companies that fit their investment criteria.

3. Due Diligence

After identifying a target company, the private equity firm conducts thorough due diligence. This process includes financial analysis, operational assessments, legal reviews, and market evaluations. The goal is to uncover any potential risks and validate the company's growth potential.

4. Deal Structuring

Once due diligence is complete, the firm negotiates the terms of the deal. This includes determining the purchase price, financing structure (equity vs. debt), and any contingencies. The firm may also negotiate management incentives to align interests.

5. Post-Investment Management

After acquiring the company, the private equity firm takes an active role in managing it. This may involve implementing operational improvements, strategic planning, and financial restructuring. The firm often works closely with the company's management team to drive growth and enhance profitability.

6. Exit Strategy

The last stage in its life cycle is exit. In general, a private equity house targets divesting its portfolio companies in some years through an exit strategy that may include the following:

- *Initial Public Offerings:* taking the company to the public by selling its shares on the stock market.

- **Strategic Sales:** Selling the company to another business that can benefit from the acquisition.

- **Secondary Buyouts:** Selling the company to another private equity firm.

Successful exits are what allow investors to realize returns and prove the ability of a firm to add value.

Case Studies of Successful Private Equity Investments

To better understand the potential of private equity investing, it is helpful to consider a few case studies involving successful investments that illustrate the strategies and possible outcomes for private equity firms.

Case Study 1: Blackstone and Hilton Hotels

In 2007, Blackstone Group acquired Hilton Hotels for nearly $26 billion in one of the largest leveraged buyouts on record. At the time, Hilton was struggling to cope with the competitive forces within its operating environment. The multifaceted approach of Blackstone was through:

- **Operational Improvement:** Streamlining processes and enhancing customer service

- **Expansion:** Moving into new markets and adding new hotel properties.

- **Brand Building:** developing the Hilton brand by way of marketing and loyalty programs.

In 2013, Blackstone was able to take Hilton public again, and the market capitalization of the company reached over $30 billion. The investment paid massive returns to Blackstone and its investors and is a great example of strategic management in private equity.

Case Study 2: KKR and Dollar General

In 2007, KKR acquired the discount retail chain Dollar General for a total of $7.3 billion. KKR saw an opportunity for expansion in discount retail as the general trend during economic downturns improved. This was addressed by the following:

- *Store Expansion:* The placement of new stores within the less privileged cities and towns.

- *Supply Chain Optimization:* Maintaining a lean supply chain by strengthening logistics and inventory management.

- *Tech Inclusion:* Adopting technology to retain customer appeal and streamline operations.

By 2018, KKR successfully took Dollar General public again, this time at a significantly higher valuation than earlier. This is another case that shows how private equity investors best leverage market trends and operational efficiencies for growth.

Case Study 3: Bain Capital and Domino's Pizza

Bain Capital invested in Domino's Pizza in 1998, looking at the strong possibility of growth in the fast-food industry. Bain's strategy was pegged on:

- *Menu Innovation:* Recreating the menu with new products, improving the quality of food

- *Marketing Campaigns:* -New marketing initiatives which increase the demand for the service or product

- *Technology Investments:* Investing in an online ordering system and improving logistics

During the time Bain was invested, Domino's saw phenomenal growth, culminate in a very successful IPO in 2004. This investment speaks volumes toward how private equity can rebrand a company through innovation and strategic marketing.

In so doing, private equity investment offers a vehicle whereby financial activists are afforded an opportunity to unlock value while simultaneously being a meaningful impetus for change in the companies in which they invest. Learn to master the sourcing and due diligence process, navigate the life cycle of an investment in Private Equity, and create the foundation for success in a dynamic market. The case studies on successful private equity investments illustrate how strategic management and operational improvements create substantial returns. Remember, as you go further along the financial path, how private equity can potentially help continue your dreams of building wealth and leaving a positive influence on the world.

CHAPTER 9
THE MONEY TRAP: RECOGNIZING AND AVOIDING PITFALLS

Possible pitfalls are important in your journey toward financial empowerment. In this chapter, you will look into common financial traps, the importance of financial literacy, and how to overcome unhelpful setbacks. By acknowledging these challenges, you can navigate your financial path with confidence and determination.

Identifying Common Financial Traps and Mistakes

1. Living Beyond Your Means

This, often enough, contributes to piling on debts, especially credit card debts. Instant gratification may override sensibilities which could enable a person to sidestep thinking about long-term consequences.

2. Neglecting an Emergency Fund

Life is unpredictable, and unexpected expenses can arise at any moment. Failing to establish an emergency fund can leave you vulnerable to financial crises, forcing you to rely on high-interest loans or credit cards when emergencies strike.

3. Neglecting Retirement Savings

Most people, particularly younger ones, do not put enough

emphasis on retirement savings. The more one postpones, the more he or she misses opportunities for compound growth and makes reaching financial security in later years more difficult.

4. Falling for Scams

Get-rich-quick schemes-most fall for these, which time and again have been proved to lead to massive losses. Be it a suspicious investment opportunity or a multi-level marketing program, the key is looking very skeptically at them and researching them further.

5. Ignoring one's financial literacy

Lack of understanding of financial products, investment strategies, and market dynamics results in poor decision-making. Most people make financial decisions based on emotions rather than informed analysis; thus, they make costly mistakes.

6. Not Diversifying Investments

Putting all your money in one type of asset or one sector exposes you to unnecessary risk. Well-diversified portfolios can protect you from losses and give you more stable returns over time.

The Importance of Financial Literacy and Education

Financial literacy is the cornerstone upon which sound financial decisions are founded. It entails understanding vital notions such as budgeting, saving, investing, and debt management. Here's why financial education is important:

Empowerment

Knowledge equips you to make informed choices about your money. When you understand how financial systems work, you can more effectively navigate them and advocate for your financial interests.

Confidence

Financial literacy provides additional confidence in handling finances. The knowledge of budgeting, saving, and investing may be less bewildering when financial decisions come your way.

Long-term Success

Better-educated individuals have long-term goals for personal finance while formulating various strategies for attaining the set goals. Therefore, this proactive attitude might be one route to accumulating wealth over a long period.

Scam Avoidance

A good financial principle will educate you on how to spot scams and frauds, therefore allowing you to avoid them. Informed people are seldom victims of such activities.

Strategies for Overcoming Financial Setbacks

Setbacks are a part of any financial journey. However, your response to such situations can make all the difference in your quest for long-term success. Here are some ways to overcome those financial setbacks:

1. Evaluate the Situation

When a setback is encountered, step back and assess the situation objectively. Know the prime reason for the problem and obtain all the information about it. The beginning of a solution comes from understanding a problem.

2. Draw Up a Recovery Plan

Make an exact plan to tackle the situation. This can be done by revising your budget, reducing unnecessary spending, or taking up extra sources of income. Setting specific achievable goals will help give direction to the process of recovery.

3. Professional Guidance

One should not feel apprehensive in approaching financial consultants or counselors. Their expertise will shed light on what and how to implement specific strategies needed for one's particular situation. Professional guidance helps you face complicated financial problems more prepared.

4. Learn from Mistakes

Every backward step is an opportunity for growth. Reflect on what went wrong; identify lessons learned. This will help make better decisions later in life and not repeat certain mistakes.

5. Financial Literacy

Never stop learning about personal finance. Read books, join workshops, and surf the net about means that interest you. The more you know, the better prepared you'll be for whatever crisis may come your way.

6. Resilient Mindset

Adversities in finance are psychologically draining. One needs to develop resilience-that after a set of adversities, one bounces back into action. Go easy on yourself, stay fixated with your goals, and remind yourself that all setbacks are temporary.

7. Build a Support Network

Surround yourself with well-understanding people regarding your goals. Friends, family members, or any community group can help in fostering encouragement, accountability, and many other valuable insights.

The ability to see and stay away from money pitfalls will take you toward your financial destiny. At higher levels of financial literacy, you are better prepared to make the right decisions whenever situations challenge you. Let's face it: setbacks offer opportunities for growth and learning; they are not roads to the end. Obstacles that get in the way can be overcome with the right strategies in place as you head out toward reaching your financial goals. Take up the journey, stay committed to your goals, and let financial activism guide you toward a prosperous future.

CHAPTER 10
THE ROLE OF CREDIT INVESTORS

In personal finance and investment, credit investing occupies an important place in diversified portfolios. Grasping the intricacies of credit investments, the associated risks, and how to leverage those for financial growth are critical for any financial activist. This chapter shall deal with the importance of credit investing, types of credit investments available, and techniques of leveraging credit for an enhanced financial journey.

The Importance of Credit Investing in a Diversified Portfolio

Investing in credit simply means a practice where one invests in debt instruments. Here, the investor lends out money to the borrower in question in return for interest payments and principal at maturity. The inclusion of credit investments in your portfolio is important for several reasons:

1. Income Generation

Many credit investments yield periodical revenues in the form of interest payments. This has become especially attractive for investors dependent on a steady stream of cash, such as retirees, or those supplementing their income.

2. Risk Diversification

Inclusion of credit investment in one's portfolio reduces the risk. Equity shows a tendency to become highly volatile; however, credit investments are less vulnerable to market turbulence. A diversified portfolio comprising equities and bonds reduces overall risk and adds stability.

3. Hedge against Inflation

Some credit instruments, such as inflation-linked bonds, provide protection against inflation. As prices increase, this increases the income from the bonds, which would keep your purchasing power intact.

4. Exposure to New Markets

Credit investing can give exposure to a range of markets, including corporate bonds, municipal bonds, and mortgage-backed securities. This might give your portfolio a lot more robustness, as well as potential for returns.

5. Preservation of Capital

Most credit investments are generally much safer than equities, especially government bonds. They can help to balance out your portfolio and protect your capital in times of economic crisis.

Other Types of Credit Investments and Their Risks

There are several types of credit investments, each with its own risk profile. It is very important to understand these types and their respective risks so that a prudent investment decision can be made.

1. Government Bonds

These are debt securities issued by national governments. They generally consist of low-risk investments, especially those from stable economies. However, these bonds usually offer relatively low returns compared with other credit investments. This involves interest rate risk-the possibility of a rate rise that will negatively affect bond prices-and inflation risk, under which the general rise in prices is likely to reduce purchasing power.

2. Corporate Bonds

Companies issue these bonds. Corporate bonds sometimes have higher yields than government bonds. However, the additional risk involves a greater chance of default-the failure of the issuer to pay interest or to return principal. This especially holds for bonds from companies that are lower-rated. Investors should check the creditworthiness of the company issuing the bond before investment.

3. Municipal Bonds

These are issued to finance public projects for state and local governments. Many of them boast tax advantages that attract investors in the higher tax brackets. However, there is a credit risk-the possibility of default-and an interest rate risk.

4. Mortgage-Backed Securities (MBS)

These securities are backed by a pool of mortgages, normally offering impressive yields. They also imply prepayment risks-if borrowers pay off their mortgage obligations earlier than scheduled-and credit risk-the possibility of defaults on the underlying mortgages.

5. High-Yield Bonds (Junk Bonds)

Owing to their lower credit ratings, these bonds bear higher interest rates. Because they will generate significant returns, on the flip side, they also entail a greater risk of default. Investors should be cautious and do thorough research before investing in high-yield bonds.

6. Peer-to-Peer Lending

A relatively new form of credit investing, whereby one lends money to borrowers directly through online platforms. Besides its potentials for attractive returns, it also embodies some multiple risks, like borrower defaults and platform risk-the possibility of the lending platform failing.

Exploring How to Leverage Credit for Financial Growth

Leveraging credit effectively can be a powerful tool for financial growth. Here are strategies to consider:

1. Using Credit Wisely

Establishing a good credit score is essential for accessing favorable loan terms. Pay your bills on time, keep credit utilization low, and avoid unnecessary debt. A strong credit profile can lead to lower interest rates on loans and credit cards, saving you money over time.

2. Investing in Income-Generating Assets

Consider using borrowed funds to invest in income-generating assets, such as rental properties or dividend-paying stocks. The income generated can help cover the cost of the debt while potentially increasing your overall returns.

3. Refinancing Debt

If you have existing debt with high-interest rates, consider refinancing to lower your payments. This can free up cash flow for investments or savings, enhancing your financial position.

4. Utilizing Credit for Business Growth

If you're an entrepreneur, leveraging credit can help you expand your business. Business loans or lines of credit can provide the necessary capital for growth initiatives, inventory purchases, or marketing efforts. Ensure you have a solid plan for repayment to avoid financial strain.

5. Investing in Education

Consider using credit to invest in your education or professional development. Acquiring new skills or certifications can lead to higher earning potential, making it a worthwhile investment in your future.

6. Building a Strong Financial Foundation

Use credit strategically to build a solid financial foundation. This includes maintaining an emergency fund, investing in retirement accounts, and diversifying your investment portfolio. A strong financial base will provide stability and opportunities for growth.

Credit investing is a vital component of a well-rounded financial strategy. By understanding the significance of credit investments, the various types available, and how to leverage credit for growth, you can enhance your financial journey. As a financial activist, it's essential to approach credit with knowledge and caution, ensuring that your investments align with your long-term goals. By incorporating credit investments into your portfolio, you can create a balanced approach that fosters both stability and growth, ultimately guiding you toward your financial destiny.

CHAPTER 11
BUILDING A FINANCIAL ACTIVIST NETWORK

On this road of financial empowerment and activism, the network cannot be more important. A good financial activist network provides support, resources, and opportunities that can make all the difference along the way. This chapter shall explore the importance of networking and mentorship, provide strategies on how to build relationships within the financial community, and highlight how collaboration can help achieve financial goals.

The Power of Networking and Mentorship

1. Access to Knowledge and Resource

Through networking, so many avenues have been opened toward immense knowledge and resources. Engaging in discussions with your peers in the financial community affords you the ability to learn from their experiences, gain insight into best practices, and maintain awareness regarding industry trends. This collective knowledge can be extremely valuable as you work your way through your financial journey.

2. Companionship and Encouragement

Joining a network of people with similar interests would provide avenues for emotional and motivational support. The process of financial activism may be substantially involving, and a community that understands your goals and struggles can make all the difference in your journey. Mentorship will provide guidance from individuals who have walked the path ahead of you, enabling you to avoid common pitfalls and stay focused on your goals or objectives.

3. Avenues for Growth

Networking allows access to newer opportunities in the form of job offers, partnerships, and possibilities of investments. Most financial opportunities come through personal relationships, so it gives a better chance of finding these if one is part of a network.

4. Accountability

A network will keep you responsible with your financial goals. The sharing of your goals with others builds responsibility to keep you focused and acting upon them. Regularly checking in with your network will give one the opportunity to measure progress and celebrate successes.

5. Diverse Perspectives

Engaging with diverse individuals enhances your insight into financial matters. Different backgrounds, experiences, and perspectives can bring new insights or creative solutions to problems that you might encounter.

Building Relationship Strategies in the Financial Community

1. Networking Events

Attend industry conferences, workshops, and seminars. Such events are ideal to come across people in the financial industry, discuss ideas, and connect with them. Introduce yourself and initiate conversations.

2. Professional Organizations

Join associations or groups having to do with finance that interest you. Most of the organizations hold events, share resources, and/or facilitate networking. Getting involved will allow you to connect to others that share your passion in financial activism.

3. Social Media

Use LinkedIn, Twitter, and Facebook to connect with financial professionals and activists in the field. Share material related to the cause, create discussions, and engage in online groups based on the specific financial problems at hand. Social media can be a big help in spreading your network and gathering much-needed information.

4. Seek Mentorship

Find models that you look up to in your field and request to be mentored by them. Clearly state your goals and intentions regarding what you wish to achieve through this relationship. A good mentor will have quite a lot to offer in terms of insight and experience on your journey of managing your finances.

5. Give Back

Perform some community service or volunteer for organizations participating in financial literacy and skills, and empowerment. In addition to your contribution to a good cause, you will also have the chance to meet other people with values and ideas similar to yours.

6. Follow Up and Stay Connected

Immediately after meeting, send a personalized note, thanking them for taking the time to speak with you. If inclined, check in on a regular basis-sharing relevant articles, inviting them to events, or simply saying hello. Relationships take some time and TLC; be purposeful in tending your connections.

7. Organize your events

Think workshops, webinars, or casual meetups over issues of money. It keeps you in an authoritative position within the community and brings in people with the desire to learn something new and network. Organizing events provides a good avenue for substantial discussions and the fostering of relationships.

How Collaboration Can Help Reach Financial Goals

1. Pooling Resources and Knowledge

Collaboration lets people pool their resources, expertise, and knowledge in striving for mutual financial goals. Whether it be through investment clubs, the co-founding of a business, or collaboration on community projects, the more people work together, the greater their potential impact and likelihood of success.

2. Risk Sharing

In financial enterprises, the roles can be shared to distribute the risks among participants. In real estate investment, for example, a partnership will reduce individual financial exposure yet allow you to take on larger projects. This can make some pretty ambitious goals achievable.

3. Diverse Skills

Every team member possesses unique skills and different ways of looking at issues. Having this talent diversity allows the creation of more multi-dimensional strategies and solutions. For instance, a team of experts from the fields of finance, marketing, and operations could develop a much more comprehensive business plan than any one single individual could have created.

4. Encouraging Innovation

Collaboration gives rise to an environment of innovation and creativity. People hailing from a diverse background and experiences can get together and brainstorm newer ideas and ways of looking at financial challenges. This may be the coming together in a collaborative spirit that may bring about the much-needed breakthrough for achieving financial success.

5. Creating Support Systems

Cooperation with others creates community and belonging. This might prove considerably helpful during hard times, as that support will encourage them to pay attention to financial goals.

6. Accountability

With others, it might be easier to hold yourself more accountable. The moment you start working on financial goals, you are automatically going to get serious to stick to it, and then you create follow-through. Regular check-ins and shared milestones can help keep everyone on track.

Building a financial activist network is one of the main parts of your journey to financial empowerment and success. Knowing the power of networking and mentorship, using successful relationship-building approaches, and accepting the dynamics of collaboration will build a team of support that catapults you toward your financial destiny. Remember, the path to financial destiny is not a solitary journey; it's enriched by the connections you make and the partnerships forged. Nurture this network, you will discover that together-so much more is possible than could ever be achieved in solitude. Move into the power of community and let it guide you on your journey toward financial activism and success

CHAPTER 12
WALKING TO DESTINY: CREATING YOUR FINANCIAL LEGACY

Financial legacy is constituted by the wealth you leave behind, the values instilled in them, and the lessons that guide the lives of future generations in their financial decisions. This chapter shall explain what financial legacy is, the ways one preserves and transfers wealth, and invite one to think about their long-lasting effect on family, community, and the world.

Understanding the Concept of Financial Legacy and Its Importance

1. Defining Financial Legacy

We define financial legacy as much more than the amount of money or assets you leave behind; it is about values, principles, and knowledge base on which your family members found their respective financial decisions. In other words, a financial legacy reflects what we believe about wealth, responsibility, and the role of money in a life well-lived. An articulate legacy may stimulate future generations to make prudent financial choices and positive contributions to society.

2. The Importance of Financial Legacy

Empowerment: A good financial legacy empowers your heirs to be wise in handling their finances. It means that you are giving them financial literacy and instilling values so as to go about the journey of life with confidence.

- *Continuity of Values:* Your financial legacy provides you with an opportunity to pass on values related to money, work ethic, and philanthropy to future generations. Such continuity might even foster a sense of purpose and responsibility among the future generation.

- **Community Impact:** A financial legacy can extend beyond your family in lending positive impact to your community through charitable causes or other initiatives that best express your value and priorities.

- **Security and Stability:** Well-planned financial heritage can give the security to your loved ones to chase their dreams, to overcome every obstacle that life throws up.

Wealth Preservation and Succession Strategies

1. Full Estate Plan

An estate is a documented way of distributing your assets after your death. It typically includes wills, trusts, and powers of attorney. A well-organized estate plan ensures that your wishes are followed, which may save your heirs from taxes and other legal complications.

- *Wills:* A will indicates how your assets are to be distributed and may name guardians for minor children. It is among the critical documents in every estate plan.

- *Trusts:* These instruments allow one to have more control over how the distributions will be made, and at what time they should be made. They enable one to avoid probate and reduce the estate's taxes, and also protect the assets from creditors.

2. The Importance of Financial Legacy

- *Empowerment:* A good financial legacy empowers your heirs to manage their finances well. You hand your heirs the keys to financial literacy and values essential for traversing through their financial journey with confidence.

- *Continuity of Values:* Financial heritage provides an avenue for passing on one's values in the use of money, work ethic, and philanthropy to the next generation. Thus, such continuity may foster a sense of direction and responsibility in future generations.

- **Community Impact**: A financial legacy doesn't have to be limited to your family. You can leave a mark in the community through the support of charitable organizations or community projects.

Security and stability are derived from a well-planned financial legacy that will afford your loved ones the security to pursue their dreams and confidence to handle whatever life throws their way.

Wealth Preservation and Transfer Strategies

1. Create a Comprehensive Estate Plan

An estate plan is a document, of sorts, that outlines how your assets should be disbursed in the event of your death. It includes wills, trusts, and powers of attorney. A properly planned estate ensures your wishes are carried out and potentially reduces your beneficiaries' taxes and frustration with the courts.

- *Wills:* A will specifies who will receive your property and may name guardians for minor children. It is the fundamental document of any estate plan.

- *Trusts:* Trusts provide greater control over when exactly your assets will be distributed and how they are disbursed. They can also serve to avoid probate, minimize estate taxes, and protect your assets from creditors.

2. Utilize Life Insurance

Life insurance serves as an effective means to protect and distribute one's wealth. It provides protection for one's loved ones from the financial consequences of one's death and allows them to pay for some expenses and sustain their lifestyles. Furthermore, the proceeds from life insurance are normally income tax-free; this makes life insurance a very effective way of transferring wealth to beneficiaries.

3. Invest in Financial Education

Equip your heirs with financial knowledge by involving them in discussions about money management, investing, and wealth-building strategies. Consider hosting family meetings to discuss financial goals, share experiences, and teach essential skills. This proactive approach fosters a culture of financial literacy and responsibility.

4. Family Financial Legacy Document

Record in this document your financial philosophy, values, and lessons learned throughout your life. This will serve as a guide to lead your heirs through and help them to understand your approach to money and what you want to be passed on. Add in stories, obstacles overcome, and how you overcame those obstacles as context and inspiration.

5. Engage in Philanthropy

Consider establishing a charitable foundation or donor-advised fund to support causes that matter to you. Philanthropy not only creates a positive impact but also sets an example for your heirs about the importance of giving back. Involve your family in the decision-making process to instill a sense of responsibility and commitment to social causes.

6. Regular Review and Updates

Life is constantly changing, and plans do too. Take the time to go over your estate plan, your insurance, and your investment strategies to ensure they constantly meet your goals and family dynamics. This proactive approach lets you adapt to any change and stay on track with your vision regarding your legacy.

Encouraging Readers to Think About Their Long-Term Impact

1. Know Your Values

some time to reflect on what is most important in your life. Consider how your spending reflects your values and the difference you hope to make in the world. Allow this to help direct and center you on what really matters.

2. Long-term Goals

Clearly define your long-term financial goals and vision for your legacy. Be it funding your children's education, giving back to charitable causes, or building a family business, having focused goals will help you stay on target and motivated.

3. Engage Your Family in the Conversation:

Discuss your financial legacy with your family and encourage an open forum on values, goals, and aspirations. This can be done collaboratively to make sure everyone is on the same page when it comes to your legacy.

4. Lead by Example

Your example is louder than words. Demonstrate those values you want your family to apply through the choices you make and behaviors concerning finances. Show them how it is done in saving, investing, and giving back, and they are likely to follow suit in these principles.

5. Consider Beyond Financial Wealth

Just like how financial wealth plays a vital role in your life, so does the non-financial part of your legacy. Your character, work ethic, and contributions to society are just as valuable. Work toward living a life whereby your legacy carries both financial and personal values.

6. Love the Process

Building a financial legacy is a lifetime process. Enjoy the learning, growing, and evolution that come with finding your financial road. Celebrate the milestones and remember your legacy is a result of commitment to your values and the impact you want to leave. Conclusion

Walking into destiny means the realization of your financial goals, but also leaving something behind that is in accordance with your vision and values as your legacy. Truly understanding the principle of financial legacy, strategies to ensure wealth preservation and transfer, thoughts about long-term impact-all come into play to lay the supportive foundation. This is your financial legacy to prove your commitment as a financial activist-to empowerment, education, and positive change. So, seize the moment and build on your legacy for the future. Allow your financial legacy to inspire others into their paths towards destiny.

CHAPTER 13
TAKING ACTION: YOUR BLUEPRINT FOR SUCCESS

As we get to the end of "The Financial Activist's Blueprint: Buy, Build, and Think Your Way to Destiny," we need to synthesize many of the insights and strategies discussed throughout this book. This last chapter gives an overview of the key takeaways, describes the step-by-step action plan to its implementation, and invites you to seize your journey into being a financial activist. Your journey toward financial empowerment and legacy creation can now begin with an action that this chapter has presided over.

Overview of Key Points Derived from the Book

1. What Exactly is Financial Activism

Financial activism involves taking responsibility for one's financial freedom, making knowledgeable choices, and contributing toward a society of financial literacy and freedom. It involves being interested in active wealth creation with full understanding and commitment toward sharing knowledge and information.

2. The Importance of a Diversified Portfolio

This is important because a well-diversified portfolio helps to overcome risk management and gives good returns. You can develop a very balanced approach with the inclusion of different asset classes such as stocks, bonds, real estate, and alternative investments to meet your financial goals.

3. Credit Investor's Role

Credit investing has an overriding importance in the case of a diversified portfolio. Understanding the different types of credit investments, their risks, and how to leverage credit for growth can enhance your financial strategy and provide additional income streams.

4. Building a Financial Activist Network

The most productive methods of personal and professional development can be attained through networking and mentorship. You will be in a position to avail valuable resources, support, and opportunities by developing your relationships in the financial community.

5. Creating a Financial Legacy

Your financial legacy is defined as the wealth, values, and life lessons passed down through generations. Through effective management regarding asset preservation and transfer, your legacy will really mirror your values and make a difference in your family and community.

6. Action

Financial empowerment shall be effected through undertaking action. You can bring your financial dreams into reality by setting clearly defined goals and developing a plan of regular steps towards attainment.

Step-by-Step Action Plan for Implementation

1. Define Your Financial Goals

Reflect on your short-term and long-term goals. Think about

what you want to achieve this year, in five years, and even longer. Write these down and apply the SMART principle on them: make them specific, measurable, achievable, relevant, and time-bound.

2. Assess Your Current Financial Situation

Give a full review to your current financial condition. Consider income, expenses, assets, and liabilities. It will provide a good view of where you are and will also pinpoint some areas for improvement.

3. Make a Budget

Create a budget that reflects your financial goals. Track income and expenses to determine where to cut costs or increase savings. A well-structured budget will put you on course with being in control of your finances and working towards your goal.

4. Build a Diversified Investment Portfolio

Invest in different investment opportunities to achieve the right diversification for your portfolio that best fits your tolerance to risk and financial goals. The combination of stocks, bonds, real estate, and alternative investments will work to diversify risk and, at the same time, increase potential returns.

5. Create an Emergency Fund

Put aside three to six months of living expenses in a separate savings account. That may be an emergency fund to fall back on for some radical changes in expenses or losses in income. It would keep you on track with your financial goals.

6. Continuous Learning

Commit to ongoing financial education through reading books, attending workshops, and following reputable financial news sources to stay abreast of market trends and investment strategies. Knowledge is power in your financial activism journey.

7. Network and Seek Mentorship

Look for active and genuine opportunities to connect with other professionals in the financial community: attend networking events, join professional organizations, and reach out to would-be mentors. The relationships being formed will help in giving valuable insights and support in the pursuit of goals.

8. Create Your Financial Legacy Plan

Create a well-rounded estate plan, detailing the distribution of your assets and the ways in which you'd like to pass on values and financial insight to later generations. Set up trusts, wills, and a charity giving strategy if needed.

9. Implement and Follow Through

Put your financial plan into action; start taking consistent actions toward your goals. Check on your progress regularly, changing strategies where needed, and celebrate your achievements along the way. Accountability is a great motivator.

10. Give Back to Your Community

As you reach all your financial goals, give a chance back to your community: share your knowledge, support local initiatives, engage in philanthropy. Not only will your contributions bring positive ripple into other people's lives, but your act also will inspire others.

Leading Your Movement as Financial Activist

As you begin, remember that financial activism isn't just about personal gain; it's about creating impact in your life and others. Each test and opportunity that will come in your life should be welcomed, seeing that with everything you do, you build upon yourself and your legacy.

1. Develop a Growth Mindset

One must approach the journey of finance with a growing mindset and not be deterred by setbacks. It is a process, and every fall is an experience to learn and rise from.

2. Inspire Others

Sharing one's experiences and knowledge with friends, family, and communities inspires others to take responsibility for their financial futures. If you inspire others to take responsibility for their financial futures, you have contributed toward a culture of financial literacy and empowerment.

3. Stay Committed

Financial activism is a lifetime process. Remain committed to the set goals, seek continuous improvement of yourself, and adjust to changed circumstances. The commitment will add value not only to yourself but also to others.

4. Celebrate Your Successes

Take the time to appreciate small successes along the way. Recognizing your growth reinforces your commitment to motivate you further in moving ahead.

Conclusion, Taking action forms the very foundation of your journey in financial activism. In all, summarizing the key takeaways-from an implementation of step-by-step action plans to being your person in financial activism-is how best you can take on the complex world of personal finance and create a lasting impact.

CONCLUSION

As we conclude "The Financial Activist's Blueprint: Buy, Build, and Think Your Way to Destiny," let us not forget to reflect on the great effect that financial activism can have, not only on personal journeys themselves but also upon the greater landscape of society. One should think of financial activism as something much bigger than a means to affluence. It is an effective movement that affords the individual a chance to take control of their financial futures, have their voices heard on financial literacy, and indeed positively contribute towards change within the community.

The role of financial activists becomes very important. One will realize through financial activism how empowerment and education are nurtured in such a way as to change lives. Your effort can be used to break down mystique from the financial concepts, challenge systemic barriers, and promote equality in access to financial resources.

Financial activism has something to do with creating a ripple-one that goes well beyond your own personal successes. It's financially educating others, being in a position to share your knowledge, giving your support to those initiatives which would contribute to there being greater economic justice, and you start to pave the way for all those coming behind you. Your commitment to financial activism empowers others to take ownership of their financial destinies and fosters a community of educated people in a better position to make positive, informed financial decisions.

As you begin to become a financial activist, remember that you are the CEO of your financial life. The ideas and strategies that you find within these pages will help you take full responsibility for your personal finance and build a lasting legacy reflective of what is important to you.

It is now time to implement this. Set clear goals, develop a plan, commit to learning continuously. Allow the challenges and opportunities to keep coming your way, with full knowledge that each step will be one toward empowerment-your own and those around you.

Share your story with other people, highlighting success stories, encouragement of open and honest discussions that build knowledge and confidence in financial literacy. Your voice matters, and your experiences can be a lighthouse of hope to help and advise others who find themselves helpless or lost as regards their life paths.

I want to encourage you to become a financial activist-with passion and purpose. The road ahead will be long and full of obstacles, yet replete with growth opportunities, learning, and impact. Owning your financial life means you will not only change your own life but also contribute to making a better, more just world for all.

Financial activism is a lifetime dedication. Be inquisitive, stay involved, and stay active for you and on behalf of others. Only together can we change the world so that financial empowerment will be accessible to all and everyone will have the means and knowledge to develop their prosperous future

ABOUT THE AUTHOR

Olojo Christiana is a passionate financial activist, entrepreneur, and also an advocate for economic empowerment for women. Firm in her commitment to financial literacy and social justice, Olojo has dedicated her life to supporting individuals and communities in making informed choices within the financial world that defines them. In fact, from life experiences, professional knowledge, and her belief in financial education, she became one of the leading voices for economic equity.

Olojo has empowered an innumerable number of people to take ownership over their financial futures. She believes financial activism is not just about personal wealth; rather, it's about creating that ripple effect which can lift a whole community. She is focused on arming others with the tools they need to begin challenging systemic barriers to advocate for their financial rights.

It is in what drives this core belief of Olojo's financial activism that everyone deserves to know and tap resources for thriving. She intersperses practical advice with a mindset of empowerment, encouraging her readers to own their potential and take actionable steps toward their financial goals.

With "The Financial Activist's Blueprint: Buy, Build, and Think Your Way to Destiny," Olojo Christiana invites you to take part in this life-changing journey into the dimensions of financial empowerment toward social change. May we strive together for a future wherein the benefits of financial freedom are no longer just dreams but a worldwide reality

www.ingramcontent.com/pod-product-compliance
Lightning Source LLC
Chambersburg PA
CBHW071109240526
45469CB00006BD/2409